About the Author

Syamal Roy holds a Ph.D. in biochemistry and trained as an immunologist at the Massachusetts Institute of Technology, Cambridge, USA. He was the chief scientist with the Council of Scientific and Industrial Research (IICB), Kolkata, India, and Former Vice Chancellor Coochbehar Panchanan Barma University (WB), India. His major research interests are immunology of infectious diseases and vaccine development. He had served as an external member of the European Vaccine Initiatives on Leishmaniasis. The current focus of his research continues infectious diseases with an emphasis on COVID-19 and serving as an emeritus scientist with the Indian Council of Medical Research at IICB, Kolkata.

Hundred Golden Leaves – Collection of Poems

Syamal Roy

Hundred Golden Leaves – Collection of Poems

Olympia Publishers
London

www.olympiapublishers.com
OLYMPIA PAPERBACK EDITION

Copyright © Syamal Roy 2024

The right of Syamal Roy to be identified as author of
this work has been asserted in accordance with sections 77 and 78 of
the Copyright, Designs and Patents Act 1988.

All Rights Reserved

No reproduction, copy or transmission of this publication
may be made without written permission.
No paragraph of this publication may be reproduced,
copied or transmitted save with the written permission of the publisher,
or in accordance with the provisions
of the Copyright Act 1956 (as amended).

Any person who commits any unauthorised act in relation to
this publication may be liable to criminal
prosecution and civil claims for damage.

A CIP catalogue record for this title is
available from the British Library.

ISBN: 978-1-80439-811-1

This is a work of fiction.
Names, characters, places and incidents originate from the writer's
imagination. Any resemblance to actual persons, living or dead, is
purely coincidental.

First Published in 2024

Olympia Publishers
Tallis House
2 Tallis Street
London
EC4Y 0AB

Printed in Great Britain

1
Hallucinatory Cosmos

Floating in the mist of void
Perceived unlimited vastness
Clouds of different size formed
Wandering happily across the sky.

Splendid beauty of the twilight
Optical experience evokes deep feeling
Freedom from chills
Crashing wave of thrills.

Horizon glitters with fleeting colors
Feel a hint of romanticism
Portal for enriching imaginative space
Endless wealth for the inner landscape.

2
Solitude

Sculpting solitude into words
Weaving threads of joy and sadness
Navigating deep inside
Rediscovering hidden past.

Trajectories of varied inner equilibrium
May be, I will write in tranquility
In silence
What I've lived through.

3
Portrayal of Unspeakable

Voyaging through inner soul
Sense of deep past
Difficult to depict, paint, and map
Sharpness of despair causing a brooding portrait.

Contours of experience can't be described
Unable to brush aside as thoughts autonomically ruminate
Vision of nightmares and dire imaginaries
Matching the resonance of inner landscape.

Product of past memories and stray ideas
Evinces images of unspecified composition
Not fitting into the inner emotional co-ordinates
Resistant to easy analysis.

Feeling of raving inner waves
Lacking defined pattern out of infinite repertoire
All are gnomic, elliptical, and exigent
Signals are ominous.

Inner life as a portal to explore mystery of existence
Proffering new revelations
Leaving with uncertainties

Issues still remain unresolved.

Quest to translate morphing inner anxieties into artful tapestry
Edging much closer for a dialogue between two conclaves
Hope for a variegated and fertile ground
New platform for a creative vision.

4
Deep Inside

Terror and horror
Ecstasy and joy
Entwined in shapeless form
Hidden somewhere deep inside.

Two distinct impulses create human existence
Unexplainable mystic form
Unresolved from time immemorial
Teeming piles of mysteries.

Philosophers expressed through the Greek deities
Apollo and Dionysus – the extreme impulses
Paired images spiraled into a chaos
Origin of artistic impulses.

Hibernate silently unceasing thoughts
Gathers strength like a windmill
Resonates with present unpleasant experiences
Proves its existence once a while.

Terrified irrational thoughts from nowhere
Kinetic interplay of chills and mumbling pain
Harness repressed pain and anxiety
An audacious goal more than doable.

5
Ode to Our Brain

Scientist Camillo Golgi made nerve cells visible
Ramon Y Cajal, a Spanish clinician, revealed it further
Smooth, triangle, stellate appearance
Many tiny hands holding one another.

Forms a white mass known as brain
Presumably site of consciousness
Reveals dancing world of beauty and ugly
Through line, color, forms, verses, and sounds.

Thrill and chill evoke sensation of opposite credo.
As in musical score of Beethoven's 9th vs Mahler's 9th
How scores on a piece of white paper
Create an internal sensation of incommunicable form?

6
Shades in a Forest

Infinite night sky above a deep forest
Soft air fans the cloud away
Million stars and different shades of night
Splashes of color looming over the forest.

Varied chromatic scale in the horizon
Optical view turned into emotional experience
Beatitude of colorful events
Became irrevocably personal experience.

Trees move in directionless breeze
Dry leaves flutter as rodents run around
Created sensuous noise
Perfect de-repression of silence.

Skittering of fluorescent flies
Gentle susurrus of waterfall
Crisp cool fine breeze
Hungry rodents yelping rustle of dry leaves.

Dew descends slowly upon tender heart
Night landscape emulates new charms
Brim with symbolic promise of artful dodge

Surge of ecstasy and happiness.

Birds near out of their nests – sunshine not too far
Half bloom color's flowers now blossoming
Incantatory celestial revelations of new imaginaries
Final page kept open to write what left unsaid.

7
A Day of the Days

Today is a day of the days
Nature showing its fury
From Edenic to apocalyptic
Abyss specter of darkness.

Sitting in a frail dingy boat
Facing the raging sea
Experiencing the vagaries of fate
Struggling to keep the boat in place.

With skill and maneuvering
Managing the carnival of giant waves
Feeling tired and exhausted
Praying to the Almighty to be on my side.

8
Inner Landscape

Life is about creating memories
Endless barrage of information
Perceived by sensory organs
Sculpt images of infinite contour.

Through complex neuronal connectivity
Embedded in space and definite context
Somewhere deep in the soul
With silent endurance.

Lasting and multiform imprint
All rambling thoughts – layer by layer
Clinching a permanent residence
No mechanism to erase.

Memory and images – two veritable metaphors
A tantalizing combination of undefined topology
Intertwined in unknown dynamics
May or may not amount to a singular aura.

Converges somewhere in an unknown horizon
Oscillate in a bewildering complexity
Stridently eclipse one's conscious command

All ethereal, beyond one's comprehension.

Wandering thoughts silently dangle
Tend to align with one's life
Thrilling blends of memory and imagination
Guiding spirit of creation.

9
Out of Old Address

Wish to blend with nomadic
New avenue for adventures
Desirous to create new resonance
A new gaze from within.

From bitter rind to sweet nut
Sour orange to sweet mango
Inglorious to glorious homilies
From silent tears to happiness.

Tides of towering hardship to joy
Chilling to inspiring openness.
Self-inflicting pain to wisdom
Imaginary with a natural smile.

Veils of darkness rends
Inner thoughts spouting wing
New value of life comes by osmosis
Made me feel royal.

A new dawn drawn to break the silence

Solitary testimony of its own
Generous palette of situation
Requiem for utopian ideas.

10
Joie-de-vivre

Iconic images within perceived sphere
Enamored with sweeping thoughts
Seeks a convenient route to navigate
Needs narrativize pictorial images into language.

Harnessing best of the present
Live with infinite clear sky with rainbow on the horizon
Enchanting, beautiful, verdant shades of green
Blooming cherries and daffodils.

Decorate soul with grace of Virgil
Imagine Dante's vision of heaven, where one would like to
live
With all finesse and delights
Demands a magic tool to navigate.

11
Gift of Silence

Silence keeps dissonant strings at bay
Scope to translate imaginative subconscious
Sculpt rumbling echoes as it flows
Into philosophical verse.

Scuttles glimmering hope
Meltingly tender pastoral inner peace
Sonic landscape of rhythm and melody in the horizon
Stimulus to articulate one's imagination into creative enterprise.

With an unfettered trove of surreal
In color, forms, and pieties
With a panache and penetrating rhetoric
Crafted a series of dioramas inside.

12
Smile

Bathe in the buttery glow of nature's treasure
Trees, butterflies, bees, flowers, and luster
Dew drops on a rose petal
And melody of songbird.

Shower with smiling moonlight
Navigate happily
Wherever mind led you
Felt amazing unwonted gaiety.

Smiling makes one powerless to empowered
Silences dreaded dream
Make peace with the barrage of variable thoughts
Anything from mundane to magical.

13
Mysticism

A wave of pervasive fog
Something like a riddle
Notoriously blurred
A portrayal of unspeakable vice.

Looking through the frosty haze
Influence is infinite
Driven by an innate and unrelenting momentum
Never-ending paradox.

14
The Sunset

The sun sets in the horizon
Behind the distant mountain
Sudden darkness evokes melancholia
Walking alone through twilight vision
Oscillating between present and long past
Enduring hidden memories of failures surface
No one to hear and no one to listen
Route is long and feels ache
Glad that I survived
Longing to fulfil my dreams.

15
My Flying Friends

Navigating in the morning civil twilight
Sunrays still invisible
Gradually, sun's upper tip visible
Time for my flying friends' visit
Tenderly sit on window bars
A silent common language eye-to-eye
Share morning greetings with biscuits
My friends depart
Assured me to return
Longing to see them again.

16
Shimmering Thoughts

With felicity, look outward
Out of gravitational orbit
Open windows of soul to let air and light in
Milieu for germinating, revving thoughts.

Sun-swept lakes and meadows
Luminous tulip color
Gazing sheep down the valley
Solitary wood bridge connecting valleys.

Children playing over the bridge
Chirruping like birds
With high-octane rhetoric
Evokes a joyous mood inside.

Each object becomes a permanent image
Pictures of paradisal nature
Impose a sense of joy
Enough to germane surreal-sounding bliss.

17
Duende

Hear the inner whisper
Feel something extra in the life process
Keeper of that space "duende"
Sits in deeper interiority
Unlike the Muse or Angels
Dark and elusive powerful force.

Unalloyed creative power an artist seeks
For inner revelation
The highest art forms
Revealed in Flamenco dancing
Matador's control of a mighty bull
Evokes emotion, anguish, and death.

Akin to Nietzsche's "Dionysian" drive
It's a power, not a behavior
Related to the life process
No one else can perceive inner dimension
Philosophers unable to explain
A real paradox abounds.

18
Contour of Inner Space

Poets imagine
Philosophers think
No one can see
Very personal identity
Contours of inner self.

Images cohere together
Echoes between memory and imagination
Surge from the inner dimension
Meaning is floundered
Seems vanished.

From ever-changing contour
With endless topology
Enjoy sensuality of simmering flames
Hold on to hope
Something better in the horizon.

19
Image of Self

Imagining a vibrant portrait of self as Peter Pan
Waking up every morning as a beady noticer
Enamored with ineffable thoughts
And emoting every dream with cosmic realm
Deftly rendered from within.

A congruent spirit of vitality
Of serenity, compassion, and oneness
Of softness and silence of endurance
With fluidity and malleability
Always shimmering with capacious thoughts.

Attaining a new realm of beauty and charm
Breathtaking empire of imaginary
Features of all paradisal realities
Cutting through the greatest delicacy
Space for cosmic vitality.

Living in a castle built in the sky
Colorful flowers in a dream garden
Tethered with charming revelations
Portrayed with a startling stride
With an exhilarating sense of pride.

Words from lips formed a hue of glaring sound
A lasting, multiform imprint
And dynamo of intellectual energy
Seeing me within myself
Tepid desire to resort toward adulthood.

20
Ode to Imperfection

Perfection and imperfection-trajectories of emotion
Formed on the mercy of circumstances
Inscribed in the primal part of the brain
Leaving behind allusions of voices and images.

Cognitions navigate hidden imaginaries
Emotes terrines of respective behaviors
A nimbus of uncertainty
Testimony of human experience.

Perfection limits the tenor of flexibility
Imbuing self-inflicting honing damaging intoxication
Perfection means nothing to strive for
Scope of life dramatically compressed.

Imperfection has its own appeal
Imperfection means still left to attain
Devoid of restrain
Pushes toward greatness.

More imperfect, more alive
Powerful beacon of motivation
Offers broad window of opportunity
Embrace simplicity of imperfection.

21
Surreal House on a Crescent

Fallen into a spell of dream
Subsumed in an iconic image of imagination
Armed with a range of thoughts
Entering the pages of unwritten book.

From my painted memories
Imagine my capacious house
Whatever the way it appears
Something baroque.

22
Wishful Thinking

Up on top of a hill
Mountain range in the horizon
Gaze wistfully
In green terrain of vegetation
With a leavening smile
Enough space to think of life and universe
Real joy – the joy of survival.

23
La-La Land

Fallen in a spell of dream
Yearning for enlightenment
Angels of Apollonian beauty
Dragged me in an ornate chariot.

A trip to a remarkable terrain
Sound of a mountain stream
Endless stream of birds, flowers, and fruits
Trees with their first blossom.

Darkness never perceived
Endless summer prevailed
Perceive baroque beauties
Oddly charming, enchantingly beautiful.

Suddenly woke up
Felt supremely confident
Full of incantatory celestial revelations
Images are waiting to be told.

24
Dream of a Dream

In me, cherish a dream
Climbing mountain
Keep gazing upwards
Looking at the heaven above.

Savage beauty of diverse wildflowers
Ornated layer by layer
Changing landscape as moving upwards
Lyrical voice of folk song from hamlets.

Mighty mountain stream follows the gravitational trail
Bending turning along the way
With daunting energy and a huge appetite
With inbuilt, enviable dynamic force.

Air of serene diligence felt
Leaving behind the chorus of voices
All by myself – a solitary testimony
Felt ephemeral, fleeting attachment.

Wide landscape of vivid dimension
Beauty and resilience
Dissolves into newfangled artistry

Perfect displays of artistic gaiety.

No footprint seen
No one perhaps ever walked
New-found inspiration
Lyrical evocation of sensual world.

Slice of the moon captured the moment
A sense of oneness prevails
Beautiful solitary testimony slid loneliness
Glimmering of joy and sadness rattled.

Standing in the crisp, restless wind
Imagination awakens
Lorca's notion of 'Denude' revealed
Emergent from the touch of death, a creative force.

25
Gentle Rain

A long spell of sweltering heat
Lacquered soil surface
A smile of fortune in the horizon
Cloud-saturated water vapor.

Clouds amorphously scattered
Harbinger immediate rain
Cool bridge enshrined
Eclipsed the sun.

Suddenly, darkened all around
Magical splash of high-octane rain
Listening to the rhythmical fall of water-drops
Often induces a dream-like mood.

Multitudes of small delights
As rendered in Chopin's musical prelude
Enjoying with silent endurance
Tone for germinating new life.

26
Behind the Curtain

Pilling childhood memories
Through adult lens
All over a dense fog
Spiraling into a chaos.

Dark memories evoke anxiety
Enforcing a sense of powerlessness
Sense of vulnerability in wandering minds
Learning to endure with unflappable silence.

Vail gradually sidled up
Mirthful eyes with mixed feelings
Darkness was a gift
What I cherish
Blessed in what I've lived through.

27
Compulsion

Senses create images
Reverberate with unknown dynamicity
Of long past and present
Of unknown dimensions and complexion.

Subdued, labyrinthine, abstract, solitary, and dynamic
Left a multiform imprint of commentary
Creates the aura of two extreme dioramas
Dark plume of compulsion or enchanting joy.

Something with deep feelings
Difficult to brush aside
Tone is earnest, often credulous
Imbuing emotional maelstrom.

28
Sensory World

Far away from wrangling
In an imaginary reverie
Cherishing a talismanic credo
Savage beauty of epical splendor.

A terrain where all four seasons live together
Emerged as a pointillist portrait
Feeling an ephemeral attachment
Fortified golden con of artistic streak.

In an altered state of consciousness
Through the portal of desire for longing
Empowered with enduring incandescent power
Decorated inner soul with votive candles.

Endless carnival of joy
Making a deal with God
For liberating and uplifting
Climbing mountain all my life.

Huge appetite for knowing the unknown
Vitality of the intellectual life
A central issue of existence
Praying for strength for the rest of my climb.

29
Peerless Trellis

Dreamy arch of a rainbow in the skyline
Glowing with startling clarity in the far horizon
Resting expression of sunshine
Choreographed a splendid beauty
Ode to an infinite richness
Nourishes inner soul.

With organic, inspirational endurance
Germane deep, beautiful, and moving experience
Riding the solitary trail of imagination
Beats a pound of schmooze
Like a fly-on-the-wall documentary.

30
Magical Potions

Perched near a fragile terrain
In a vortex of gloomy narrative
Darker side of life's contour
Having a quiet dystopic.

Cauldron imbues guiding spirit
Conjured a rhythmic and melodic landscape
Feeble attempt to endure joy
Unending craving for a bigger life with candor.

Tale of two extremes
Powerful spectrums of revelations
Playing out invisibly off the page
Out of past and into the future.

Making peace whatever comes
Flexing ambitious appetite
Memory nudge with swirls and whorls
Here lies the nucleus of creativity.

31
Painting Thoughts

Ordeals of the past and parlous future
Uneven mix of dynamic process
Struggle to combat with changes
Fragile sense of longing.

Testifies follies and vulnerabilities
Negotiating with multiple through
Cloud of tension, uneasiness, and frustration
With a wildly distorted array of hallucinations.

Flinching emotional acuity
A portrayal of barren, derelict
Oscillates forbiddingly in the complex world
The eternal inevitable of our lives.

Turning prism to see things from different points
Spinning images rotating continuously
Thoughts mirror a fresh perspective
To see life with a new candor.

New sensation ginned up with silent endurance
Inner life – a maelstrom of sensibility
Stimulus to fuel new ideas

Germane a fresh thought.

A state of arousal
Theme of love and longing pervades
Liberate the body from the spider net
With each breath, a crashing desire to live.

32
Monolith of Memory

What I write today will remain
Time will roll over it
Light will come and go
Will be continuously revealed.

Returning to the past again and again
What behind is not lit
Cannot bring back what is gone forever
Iridescent sunset.

Like the tenor of despair and hope
Rigorously paired, all condensed
Testament of ephemeral nature of living
Love and to be loved.

Curtain billowing out of the window
A breath of fresh air
Act of celebration and carnival of joy
Looking for enough endurance and space.

33
Portal of Imagination

Lit votive candles
Starting a new journey
With glimmering joy, dreams, and memories
With mirthful eyes with boyish geniality
With enduring incandescent
Golden aura in the horizon
Brace liberties of creative freedom
Wishing showers of cheerful longevity
Learning to live with glee.

34
Defrosting Memories

Moored to a brio of roaring sea
Hovering over the fading memories
Distinctively meandering portrait
Frenzy atlas of the mind.

Trembling over the edge of void
Pondering equanimity to erase eeriness
No machine to keep erasing itself and making new ones
Obvious realities surfaced.

Endless array of giant waves in a raging sea
Ragged emotion glimmers with the power of each wave
Amply a touchstone for transition
Splashes of a new credo.

Series of magical doorways opened
Momentarily energized
Let's live for today
Not for tomorrow, because it is unknown.

Dynamic sound of waves unfailingly joyful
Glittering sunrays avowing cheerful resilience
Transformed solitary imagination to a broader canvas

Drooling over the fabled past.

Everything appeared as fresh
A multitude of small delights
Leaving behind a dark cavern
Peeping through the window to see the wonders.

Blueprint of solipsism aphoristically gyrates
Lyrical evocation of the sensual world
Honoring the memories left
The ones are charismatic with lasting appeal.

35
Unfettered Labyrinth

Stunning autumn sunset in the horizon
Creeps a trail of creative vision
Glistens a man-made paradise on the earth
Much as in "Kubla Khan."

Imbuing Coleridge's opium-induced dreamy arena
Emoting a hallucinatory cosmos
Multitudes of metaphors and imaginary
Mysterious feeling of own being.

An arrogant ambition of immortal creation
Recounting Aldous Huxley's psychedelic experience
Under the influence of mescaline
Far away from the perils of the surroundings.

Experiencing invisible resonance inside
A portal from mundane to magical
Subsumes intolerable life of ordinary living
Route to the course of new life.

Getting into the sub-conscious
Subtle buttery hermetic hip-hop
Like Alice's journey into rabbit hole

A method to unlock imagination.

Whetting appetite for similar dream
Quest for iconographic images
Lilting beyond blurred boundaries
Relief from perpetual depression.

36
Goofy Dream

Dreamy arch of rainbow in the horizon
Glowing with startling clarity
Resting expression of sunshine
Choreographed a splendid beauty
Passionate lilting warbling
Rendering vibrant baroque splendor
Nourishes inner soul.

Act of an organic inspiration
Variegated mythical resonance
Germane deep, beautiful array of excitement
Riding a solitary trail of imagination
Looks out into an artful collage
Longing for imagined delight.

37
Words

The smallest unit of language
Most meaningful element of speech or writing
Different meanings at different levels
Sometimes partly expressive as a single entity.

Lively sentence needs combinations to discern
Form pictorial imaginary to an artful story
From the riveting tale of a cherished dream
From sublime music of the sphere and of infinity.

Eyes scan the words
Brain recognizes them
As a pattern of neural activity
Evoked stream of magical thoughts.

38
Soft Blanket

In a poignant, fragile life
Nimbus of uncertainty persists
Seeks a carapace for inner comfort
Like warm days of spring.

Meltingly tender inside with overpouring freshness
Stuffed with cosmic and elemental edge
Drifts with all fair and grace
In a surreal-sounding sheepish haute.

Life moves out of liminal realm
New place is not the same as it was
Juxtaposed between a lovelorn spirit and uncertainty
Hovers between expressed and unexpressed thoughts.

Uneasy combination of conflicting imaginary
Greatest ring of truth on the earth
A rousing testament of mysticism
Full of paradox.

Past comfort and current struggle widen
Internal mixed cues lurk
A temporal mismatch

Needs to dispel fog.

Confluence of floating totem of life
Revealing the invisible specter of duality
Mystery and horror
Solitude and companionship.

Triumph and trouncing
Illuminate and obscure
Blessings and curses
Culminating a distinctive conflict.

Between the chasm and endless relaunch
Experiencing suffering makes a better person
Pushes into an altered state of consciousness
Something lit within the wandering mind.

Canvas of intellectual prism enshrined
Offers a glimmer of hope and comfort
Lies the world of art and literature
Resting under a soft blanket and listening to Bel-Canto aria.

39
Eden to Chaos

Darkened portal in human progress
Slipping through a darkened door
Bemoaning the future of the human race
A drip-drip-drip
Bleary intimacy of Eve and Adam
Roused admonition
Impending human evolution.

Proselytizing wangle exercise of Lucifer
Offered forbidden fruit from the 'Tree of knowledge'
Carried seed for reproduction
Fueled multitudes of emotion
Rebelled against imposed restriction
Being unknown that joy may overweigh the pain.

The pair gained unwavering mystic power
Mind touching the mind
Brazen hounds of love swoon
Evoked crashing wave of uncontrolled intimacy
Biological immorality ensured
Expelled from the 'Garden of Eden'
Journey from paradise to chaos.

40
Praise of Math-Poetic Horizon

Discord to consider mathematics and poetry as a pair
Mathematics echoes in the orbits of poetry
Pervade in a broad range of poems
Set of defined motifs amid pastiches.

Incantatory union of two in rhythm and imaginary
Both poetry and mathematics use 'infinity'
Both use—fewer amulets than any other written forms
Express the power of imagination, the one in the heart and the other in the head.

Sonnets express great thoughts within limited lines
As in quatrains of Persian algebraist Omar Khayyam
And so, in Tennyson's "In Memoriam"
Poetic form of Haiku expresses beautiful thoughts in seventeen words.

Both spark beautiful strobe of any truth
Express of natural emotions in simple language
But poetry more ethereal than mathematics
Subject of sensational expose.

Ineffable beauty of each one

Embedded in spaces and context majestically
Finding patterns out of infinite possibilities
Fusion of two created scope for new imaginative grandeur.

41
Hourglass

Dynamic shifting paradigm
Endless carnival of extraordinary images
Adding to the mental library
Evokes resonant arcane portraits.

Fleeting tangy waves of emotion
Dissolve into a wide-ranging ensemble
Recurrent reveries of existence
Make peace with whatever be the thoughts.

42
Dilettante Poet

On a boundless summer day
Passionate warbling
Unwavering aspirations hovering
Longing to express nuanced imaginaries.

Structure, pattern, symmetry – something divine
Startling array of atonal themes
Feeble attempt to give a shape
From mundane to sublime.

43
Random Thoughts

A gnawing creative cry
Something aspiring and elegant
Levees of passions and paradoxes
With full of ineptitude.

Where to go from here – I wonder
Ventures into an audacious goal
Success is always questionable
Until the finish line is crossed.

World seemed under grand complexity
Shades of hope and despair in tandem
Pain generated a brand of magic
Taught me how to survive.

44
Dualism

A daunting question hangs in the air
Tale of two key traits in human
Live side by side in silent endurance
One on stage and the other in the audience.

Extraordinary mix of tantalizing combination
Enticing portrayal of metaphysical dualism
Melts into glissandos of finely varied emotion
Squalls of unpredictable outcome.

Perceived their sphere of influence
A mysterious paradigm of its kind
Harmonizing the two – an engrossing storyline
Captivated the origin of conflict.

'Tree of knowledge' of good and evil
Singular totem of life stream
Two extremes floating in a void
Embodies the beginning of conflict.

Zarathustra – central to ideas of dualism
Emblem of good and evil
Tempestuous gains of truth

Spectrum of human condition.

Nietzsche's intellectual introduction
Athenian tragedy – an art form of duality
Two "drives" rational and irrational
Named after Greek deities, Apollonian and Dionysian.

Two interwoven creative energies
The coupling of the rational and the irrational
Entry into a dystopic world of fragile terrain
Through which great art is born.

Renaissance master Michelangelo
Biblical narrative in the Sistine Chapel
Adam almost touching hand of God
Perfect frozen creation hinted deeper meaning.

God's arm dissolves to Adam's brain
The convergence hub of information
Site for creative process
Sovereign impulse governs one to its will.

45
Rain

Sweet summer rain
Upheavals freshness in life stream
Beacon of boundless cosmic vitality
Endless hours of unalloyed joy
Dipping into surreal subconscious.

Moist breeze unfolds pages
Felt immensely high
Nimble symphony of creativity
Recipe for reinvention of sonnets
Clarion of visible brightness.

46
Surreal Images

Stream of meteor in the sky
Something overtly charismatic
Evokes crashing wave of desire
One of divine likeness.

Images bubble up the imagination
Resonate with the inner landscape
Enduring the allure of creation
With all fair and grace.

With baroque extravagant
Utterly, blissfully, and restful
Nourishing inner soul
Steady barrage of gaiety parable.

47
Luscious Imaginaries

Endless spell of voices and images
Boundless pleasure of vivid dimension
Feelings of personal ownership over the images
Combining and recombining to give way to a romantic tale.

Flurries of resonating inner voices
Whatever coming to the surface through kaleidoscopic thinking
Avenue of fulfilling ambition and fantasies
Opportunity to choose topic without limitations and imposition.

Glamorous whisper of pristine celestial bodies
An ardently charming to rob unpleasant memories
Impelled to write literary trellises from silent tears to ecstasy
With piercing gaze and startling clarity.

World of bright canvas, source of fresh oxygen
Ready with artist's pencil, brush, and chisel
Creating everything loveable and valuable
Enough reverie for rest of the climb.

48
Faustian Bargain

It was a dream of the dreams
Wandering in the moonlit Garden of Eden
Sparkling lakes and rolling meadows
Richly hued with flowers and foliage.

All are lively with truth and hope
A confluence of gaiety and glee
Peaceful destination than imagined before
Perfect ambience of a nimble creative energy.

Artful dream was fleeting
Leaving behind all the thrilling joy
Surrender to the degrading life stream
Returned into the tedium of incomprehension.

Resonating between cradle and grave
Two things side by side
Profound themes of human existence
Associates with a new meaning.

Search to fulfill twin obsession
Longing for knowledge and lust for life
Slowly curtain getting down
Traded "Faustian bargain" to fulfill my dream.

49
Self-Discovery

Navigating into ill-lit childhood
Creating a structure of days long past
Dwelling with many past feelings
Solitary testimony, no one can perceive.

Mundane memories became monstrous
Close examination makes more vicious
Mistrusting own memories
All are mine, a stranger.

A struggle between two divided consciousness
Battle of worrying penchant
Unfettered howl of vulnerability
Can't disown the ones still vivid.

What senses perceived
May be wrong person in the right place
Getting sucked into the anxiety vortex
Experiencing shades of awe.

Despair and greyness swirl around
A portrayal of grief and unspoken sorrows
Attempting to pacify lingering numbness

Reconstructing past and deconstructing feelings.

Invisible, un-Edenic world of childhood
Cannot move forward
Mysterious modes of my own being
Past echoes in my present living.

Getting older, surveying through the prism of life
Translating realities into ecstasies
Experimenting with living and loving
Hosting last hurrahs to live a meaningful life.

50
Mental Portfolio

All these years
Walking over barren soil
Tired with perishing dryness
Arching laments of failures.

A neglected child hidden within
Whisper of nested traumas
Dark account of man's obsession with the past
Dwelling with radical realities.

Life thrown into curve ball
But the joy I crave
Try to find a ray of sunshine
Arch of rainbow in mental landscape.

Deeply thinking about Hilary Mantel's cliché
"Great art emerges from great suffering."
Sartre's famous quote, "Existence precedes essence."
A central tenet of evolutionary thinking.

Taking refuge to William Blake's adage
"The fools who persists in his folly will become wise."
Recalling few lines of poem by Jamaluddin Rumi

"If you are irritated by every rub, how will you ever get polished."

Like Susan Sontag wrote down
What she saw with chilly detachment
Toward a painful longing
These are edifying philosophical ardor.

Took refuge to write a poem
Reimaging hope with moony innocence
Trying to form another life
Ready to wait infinitely in a finite life.

51
Dark Conclave

Portrayal of a powerful alien being inside
An entity of undefined dimension
Created haunting abyss
Disturbed the mental paradise.

Invisible, inaccessibly foggy, eponymous demon
Dissolves into unspecified haze
Tales of poignant fragility
Enduring self-inflicting pain.

Misplaced emotional co-ordinates
Nestled oddly between divided consciousness
Unbecoming moments
Sliding between two ineluctable dissimilarities.

Nobody wants darkness in album
Resilience to traumas increases the realization to survive
Silently leavened by the nimbus of hope
Promise of glimpses of the world beyond.

52
Fractured Mirror

Dystopic tale of inner torments
Seemingly a dark plume of smoke
Evokes mysterious Dionysian tropes
Emerged from the haze of death.

Solitary journey towards self-knowledge
Every day, a new call to survive
Curated an erudite sensibility
Gliding to the next stage.

Awaken stream of consciousness
Opportunity for something different
A delicate avenue to step outside
Looking for the bliss of paradise.

53
Inner Parable

Invisible communication between self and self-counterpart
Floating in a void, beyond an invisible cloud
Intertwined with the mesh of emotion
Of past suffering and current struggle.

Forgotten past is not the past
Juxtaposed with twists and turns of memory and time
Narratives of greed, lust, and suffering
Shaped by something one did not choose.

Self-counterpart, the existence of mine
Worthy of untwisting, forbiddingly complex landscape
Realized that life was imperfectly grown
Seemingly a new edge of consciousness.

Very hard to open the window shutter
Life an epitaph of revelatory inner voyage
Journey of unpacking memories
Continue to delve so long legs cease moving.

54
Invisible

Trying to make sense
The one's terrifying me
Physically, it does not exist
Impose suffering with silent endurance.

Trying to write about the inner world
Like to tell but lack the courage to tell
Nobody has my memory
Nobody has my dream.

Revealing the darkest corner
To prove things exist
Beneath the surface of consciousness
The invisible portrayal of life.

Restless search for answers
Looking away is still harder
Trying to move to the next stage of existence
Like the journey of Dante's soul.

55
Sense of Self

Passing through the blizzards
Painting lonely voices
In the mist of suffocating darkness
Many of these are of dissonant strings.

Difficult to talk about suffering
Hearing voices never heard before
Passing through follies
Longing to find the key to set free.

Enduring pain – a road to be wise
Darkness gradually starts spouting wings
Thoughts awaken imagination
New life became best friend.

56
Inner Conclave

Contending with past is self-denial
Deliberate attempt to hide
A bit of bubbled life
Why have they come alive now?

Carnival of unpleasant flashbacks
Afraid to express personal truth
Looking away is still harder
Worth illuminating these shadows.

World of invisible and inward thoughts
Feel driven to seek out at a greater level
A long journey with tired legs
Trying to make use of time left.

Inner life sprang a maelstrom of sensibility
Searching words to express howling agonies
So many stories waiting to be told
As a revelation of a pale view of life.

Damaged soul search for the one that caused injuries
Hovering in all directions
Desperate to get a therapeutic purge
Reimaging what is possible.

57
Frozen in Time

Trying to live on own terms
Crafting beautiful small moments
What's worth framing
Enduring pleasure of abiding thrills.

Strident curiosity takes far from the shore
Thinking all the unthinkable
Fine touch of a chisel giving completeness
Feelings of self-esteem.

Blending a triptych of love, truth, and wisdom
Cosmic vitality springs
Turning prism to see something divine
Portrait of creative vision ripples.

A breath of freshness
Unflinching corporeal thoughts
Imbued with existential dimensions
Inner soul edging toward a new dimension.

58
Spectrum

Seemingly disjointed images finely honed
Mostly suffocative, but a few are beautifully rendered
A bitter task to pull a deeper glimpse of interiority
What eyes had seen and what mind retained.

Wave of old haunts of bygone days glistens
Rustle of grass to rippling despair
Aching laments came to reveal itself
Portrayal of a structure of old days.

Feeling of despair has existential meaning
Seed of a broader canvas
Enriches greatly if one finds inner meaning
Emerges as a source of light in the dark.

Act of imagination echoes in memory and vision
A compelling desire to survive
Aiming in the process of remaking
Behold moment's pain with a kaleidoscopic sense of possibility.

Hedging from mundane narratives into pompous omen
Needs self-crafting sensory provocation

Remaking tides in own sonnet
A new experiment in living and self-loving.

New thoughts surface with an intensifying gaze
Trying to construct a shrine of gaiety
With daunting energy and appetite
Making canvas more "Monet" than eyes can perceive.

59
Singular Sensation

To live a life far beyond dreams
Gliding away from the allegorical theme
Forging bygone thrilling small moments together
Enamored for longing in the space and context.

Ready to paint golden thoughts
Of brightness, peace, and beauty
Writing to an imaginary lover
Something surreal, reverie and poetic.

All set for an incredible journey
Enjoying beauty in the humblest things
Longing for a key to a lively terrain
Unpacking new hope to nourish inner life.

Moving along the spectrum of the elusive whole
Every space in between sun and earth
With a blend of invigorating helf and poise
Quest to find a place to live with grace.

60
Imaginary

Pondering romantic thoughts in a dream sequence
Delightful and arresting vision of heaven
Everything illustrates an Olympian quality
Unwonted gaiety in inner life.

Timeless stretches beyond the field and mountain range
Far distance into eternity
Greeneries glow, and shadows are erringly bright
Meandering splashes of the iridescent landscape.

Nymph stomps through songs
Listening from a distant space
Vanguard of picturesque beauty
Like to tell stories to make others happy.

61
Behind the Mask

Inner follies evince in images and words
Felt alone, abandoned away from the living world
Blurred boundaries dissolve into humdrum realities
Reached a low ebb of howling agony.

Forgotten scenes of the past became alive on a chilly night
Most are unwelcome than others
Triangle of sadness, draught, and conflict
Grey shades of tragic narratives.

Disturbed thoughts ferried far away
Spell of sleeplessness
Destabilized shades of awe
Dark blips along the horizon to a vanishing point.

The experiences are intensely personal
Drifts through the tumult in a haze
Parade of convoluted thoughts
Cloud of tension and uneasiness.

A memoirist coming to terms with own memories
Connecting seemingly two distinct realms
Tired legs navigating to a new address

A way of self-discovery with new energy.

Nimble creative energy emerged touched by death
Feeling a new force that doesn't have before
Translating feelings into words
Joining 'Ars Poetica' to be a productive being.

62
In Praise of Surreal Dream

Thinking visually a trail of imaginative happiness
Empty head with infectious vibrancy
Walking happily down the terrain of incorporeal void space
Going far beyond the visionary landscape.

Exhilarating, beautiful, and articulate aspiration
Endless wealth of wonders
Embalm of amazing parable
Weaving indelible images deep inside.

Verdant shades of glorious Mont Blanc in the far horizon
Multicolored, sun-dappled extraordinary landscape
Portraying an invisible marvel in the mental triptych
Source for an endless barrage of creative verse.

Fertile arable land, sparkling lake, and humming breeze
Lush greeneries with arresting landscape
Doves fluttering up and down
Birds building their nests.

Natural artistry elicits magical smile
Enduring pleasure and illumination
Inspiring source of therapeutic purge

Longing to find a key to set romanticism to last forever.

Butterflies of divine color sucking nectar
Chirruping birds inviting their mates
Nesting in the Edenic bliss of paradise
Unquenched appetite for the creation of lasting appeal.

63
Beyond Dream

Lit votive candles – a portal of imagination
Starting a new journey
With glimmering joy, dreams, and memories
With mirthful eyes with boyish geniality
With enduring incandescent
Golden aura in the horizon
Brace liberties of creative freedom
Wishing showers of cheerful longevity
A way forward.

64
Spectrum

Pain without yelping pain of the inner world
Perpetual waves of spine-chilling thoughts
Difficult to depict and unable to ventilate
Involuntary journey of the nihilistic abyss of despair.

Difficult to struggle with metaphors hovering in a vacuum
Caught up in a tangle of darkness, enough to eclipse creation
Wading through an anxiety vortex needs a way out
Slowly entering the direction of duress.

Unknown entity of undefined shape and size dominating
Life is punctuated by a dystopian ambience
Breaking the soul into pieces
As if the earth tumbles under the feet.

Power of the inner world seems infinite
Two separate lives, one inside and the other outside
Two distinct parallel worlds of consciousness
Difficult to come to terms with a destructive inner self.

With fragile but visceral sense of longing
Between the sun and earth, search of friends
But never found

Realized that exit has no future.

In this wail of anguish, writing is the only avenue
Coexisting with a radiant appetite for living
Even considering the Faustian deal
To remain alive, to love and to be loved.

65
Down the Rabbit Hole

Alien thoughts overarched unheeded warning
Emanating from nowhere
Disturbing, serene inner conclave
Wave of stormy, desolate landscape.

Feeling dimness in golden light
Mirroring a fractured understanding of life
Walking alone in the midst of presumably happy majority
Hauling sensation of deep silence.

Continued to dwell with a quotidian existence
Touching frenzy nadir too closely
Living in the midst of oddly divided consciousness
More and more difficult to endure.

Emanating unkindness from inside
Mounting resonances of apocalypse
Worst whisper of death
Curveball lives beyond the limits of endurance.

Tussle with the inner self
Metaphoric embodiment of central conflict
Genesis of unspeakable turmoil

Petering out what it was and what it is now.

Hopelessly trembling in the void
Lying in an empty and ethery tearful state
Overshadowing the moments with unease
Sitting in a frail boat waiting for the storm to cease.

Trying to keep buoyant in the rippling despair
Learning to live with uncertainty
Inner mystery seeps into writing
Avenue to discover about self.

Like the final movement of Mahler's ninth
Bouncing between haves and have-nots
Ruminating Joycean meditation to set a new tone
Inscription of the hall of Delphi cliche self-knowledge.

Darkness in all directions-looking for a refuge
Self-generated feeble attempt to restore space
On the first warm day of spring
Feeble attempt to reform what has been presumably deformed.

Diverse inner moods and voices
Overwhelming experiences reveal a new truth
Orchestrates pixels of joy and nimble creative energy
Navigating through a rabbit hole into treasure island.

66
Out of Cul-de-sac

Glum admission of mind-spanning anguish
Invisible chill in the middle of blazing summer
Reimaging new hope seems far off in the distance
Unable to exalt neurosis into something thrilling.

Lingering sorrow destroyed inner confidence
Years of baying unproductivity
Living embodiments of unappealing metaphor
Surrounded by perfect helplessness.

Overburdened grid to the point of failure
Marked by the widespread sensitivity to misery
Inner landscapes reflected in the real-life canvas
Bemoaned sequel of unending duress.

Each moment is taking a new resonance
Reflects a deeper truth of human experience
Somatic shivering forcing to re-think
Each breath generates a sharp desire to live.

Feeble attempt to restore the lost space
With all uncertainties and fierce vulnerability
One will die inside, if tries to hide

Aria of new vision to liberate.

Standing between sunset and light to come
Hideous shades of many moods and many voices
Artists have no choice but to express their lives
Aspiration for a solo journey toward the unsullied paradise.

67
Flipping Through

Vivid journey of stream of consciousness
Slyly piecing thoughts, the charming and moony prudishness
Nimble narratives of a dream-like world
Filled with birdsong, a breeze, soft kisses and love.

Panorama of new landscape enthralled by connections and distances
Parlance of a complex imaginary inducing both awe and disquiet
Subtle monologue of diverse experiences
Painting thoughts into a continuous linear narrative.

Luminous, riveting, charming and likeable
Enters an ardent literary affair
Gradual unfolding, moment by moment
Something not to be interrupted.

In tune with the ever-changing color
Thrilling blend of pleasure and darkness
Juxtaposed between tutelary spirit and a cautionary tale
An ode to depart from a regular day-to-day tale.

68
Your Mind Knows You Don't

Hovering inside the pervasive fog
Written with invisible ink, both conformity and denial
Swung between agonized sobbing and passive despair
Influence is infinite, power to maneuver is negligible.

In a murky corner, mysteriously dowels mysteries
Tension arises from the irreconcilability
Two separate lives, one on stage and other in audience
Life is divided, immensely precarious.

Exploring terrains of own torments
Repertoire of anxiety, hope and possibilities
One can wave an imaginary flag
Reimaging what is possible.

A helpless child deep inside
Hibernating as a dry twig unattended
Soil needs proper moisture to support new life
Rarefied with nutrients fortified with love.

Bending emotional co-ordinates outwardly
Gradually drifting away from the haze
Painting a vivid route for a new journey
Making peace with the two punctuated worlds.

69
Moon in a Cloudy Sky

Passage of time winnowed memories of long past
Dwelling with hidden aberrant embodiments
Subtle dysphoria reactivates hidden feelings
Contours of traumas surfaced as a haunting portrait.

Traces of recursive thoughts resonate disorderly
Chasms of disturbed emotions
Unable to walk away from these feelings
Accompanied always as a gloomy companion.

Working harder to push dark thoughts away
Remained unresolved all these years
Resurfacing time to time from inner depth
Ceases to resolve as time passes by.

In the world of memory and oblivion
Inner darkness spouting wings
Opens terrines of fundamental uncertainties
End results of a life-long obsession.

Mysterious allure of well-worn aphorism
Echoed a new way to grasp an exclusive space
Passage of the inner world outwardly for poetic rupture

Longing attempt to record the inner tenor with a pen.

Wishing hermetic recourse for the freedom
Desire to float in a void of dream color
Not for optical experience
But for emotional schmoozing.

70
Emotional Maelstrom

Images recorded automatically
Steadily accumulates in a primal place
One is simply a bystander
Always a chance, not a choice.

Mixtures of many tides
Leading to an unknown mix of hews
Reshaped personality and course of life
Leaves one non-plussed.

An account of inner life and struggle
Keeps one awake and tinkers during sleep
What one achieves inwardly, comes outwardly
Something organic but connected to reality.

Happiness robed by unpleasant memories
Waves of natural gifts
Arresting the surge of ecstasy
Nested inside the casket.

Desire to make sense of new resonance
Truth may be elusive
Experiences are real
Let these flow on their own.

Trying to harness the best
Vulnerability offered an exclusive space
Learning to live with uncertainties
Is it Achilles Heel or a nucleus for new imagination?

71
Let It Until

Living under the aerial symphony of dark cloud
Navigating to discover self but don't find
Seeking inner strength to dispel fog
Searching for new rhymes and resonance.

Desirous to perceive a parade of breath-taking imaginaries
A trove of surreal and philosophical verse
Serene new world of pastel colors
Cherishing a new dream journey.

Wishing to be in a chariot pulled by fiery horses
Reach heaven to receive the grace of the goddess
Blessed with infinite knowledge and wisdom
To start several new beginnings.

With a radiant appetite for the joy of learning
Enough to illuminate murky corners
Let the emotion flow on its own
And always be hungry to ponder new dreams.

72
Remaking

A new way forward to realign with wind
Leaving behind qualms of the blue period at bay
Finding a more generous palette of feeling
Something overtly charismatic in rhymes and resonance.

Looking at life through a different lens
Two concurrent existence – black and white binary
New adjustment got through
Something in the psyche, produced oneiric effects.

Abound flurry of bright color of summer
Soothing cool color of spring or soft color of winter
Defying lurking shadows for the beauty of shamanic vision
Picking up the trail of creative enterprise.

Clarion of visible brightness in lifestream
Tantalizing stimulus to fuel new ideas
Vivid realization of duality in human life
Resistant to easy analysis.

Arts, anguish, and emotion
As Lorca appears in Dionysian drive
Experimentation with hidden abstraction and imaginary
Imaging truth, hope, facts, and glaring possibilities.

73
Rise and Shine

Amid Knightian uncertainty and greyness
Dynamic mesh of emotion and conflict
Dionysian intrusion surreptitiously re-shaping inside
Impelled to create something admirably prolific.

Ramped up by a chisel through an evolving logic
Became a different person with distinct epochs
A virtue set apart from ordinary men
Conjuring trajectories of lasting appeal.

Going back to the point of remaking choices
Cultivating a sense of uniqueness
Ceding a space for obsession with poetry
Ambling pleasure enough to overcome regressive thoughts.

As a portrayal of life's new journey
But time is finite, like the hourglass
No way to escape the paradox that weaved our lives
Central point of our natural world.

74
Musing

Dreamy, drowsy eyes
Mist of surreal thoughts
Bright full moon on the horizon
Cloud in the vast sky passing by
Obscuring glimmerings of brightness
Hope and folly side by side
Twain's trysts of human life
Embodies dual layers of two dimensions
Never-ending poignant fragility
Adage to the reality.

75
Corporeal Vision

Night sound of rain forest
Gentle susurrus of waterfall
Crisp air, intoxicating and redolent
Surreal amusement of unforgettable latitude.

Mushroom like clouds hop in and out of sight
Something disorderly ordered and dynamic
Far horizon, the silvered skyline
Iconic image turned to landscape.

Fueling something mundane to magical
Of unknown dimensions and depth
Nourishing ode to infinite richness
Embracing the abstract, the surreal and sublime.

76
The Golden Beauty

Under blue-sky, sun-splashed infinite lake
Morning dew yet to evaporate
Brisk wind roughing the water
Endless soft stream of glittering waves.

Inner self alludes as a painter
Painting startling bright splashes
Spectacular, surrealist tinge vision
Golden con of artistic streak.

State of earnest wondering
Floods of memory unloosed
Blurring the boundary between life and art
Embodiment of ceaseless euphoria.

Blending of beauty and solace
Smallest moment acquires extraordinary meaning
Envisioned as abode of peace
Praising the ephemeral, the fleeting attachment.

77
Heartbeat of the Wild

Love for adventure
Exploring dark dizzying silent wilderness
Glowing stars in the far horizon to a vanishing point
Opportunity to explore endless secrets.

Portraiture beyond imagination.
Attempt to a new adventure
Looks for the heaven above
Opportunity to communicate with the Lord.

In the sweeten solitude of wild
Feeling reborn in its wake
In the sound of silence
A storehouse of delight.

Vivid state of reality of another kind
Darkness is a source of new adventure
Man's search for meaning of life
Realized that being in the world is ultimate reality.

78
Muse, Angels, and Duende

Hear the inner whisper
Feel something extra in the life process
Keeper of that space – the "Duende"
Sits in deeper interiority
Unlike the Muse or Angels
Dark and elusive force.

Unalloyed creative power, an artist seeks
For inner revelation
The highest art forms
Revealed in Flamenco dancing
The way matador controls a mighty bull
Evokes emotion, anguish, and death.

Akin to Nietzsche's "Dionysian" drive
It's a power, not a behavior
Related to the life process
No one else can perceive the inner dimension
Philosophers unable to explain
Paradox abound.

79
Wishful Thinking

Up on top of a hill
Mountain range on the horizon
I gaze wistfully
In green terrain of vegetation.

With a leavening smile
Enough space to think of life and universe
Joycean meditation on desire
Wish to live beyond dream.

80
Peerless Trellis

Dreamy arch of rainbow
Glowing with startling clarity in the far horizon
Resting expression of sunshine
Choreographed a splendid beauty
Nourishes inner soul.

With organic, inspirational endurance
Germane deep, beautiful, and moving experience
Riding the solitary trail of imagination
Beats a pound of schmooze
Like a fly-on-the-wall documentary.

81
Painting Thoughts

Ordeals of the past and parlous future
Uneven mix of dynamic process
Fragile sense of longing
Struggle to combat with changes.

Testifies follies and vulnerabilities
Negotiating with multiple thoughts
Cloud of tension, uneasiness, and frustration
With a wildly distorted array of hallucinations.

Flinching emotional acuity
A portrayal of barren, derelict
Oscillates forbiddingly in the complex world
The eternal inevitable of our lives.

Turning prism to see things from different points
Spinning images rotating continuously
Thoughts mirror a fresh perspective
To see life with a new candor.

New sensation ginned up with silent endurance
Inner life – a maelstrom of sensibility
Rarefied to generate deepest resonance

Under the prismatic sun.

Solitude as an anchor of creative practice
Stimulus to fuel new ideas
Germane, a fresh thought
A state of arousal.

Theme of love and longing pervades
Liberate body and being from the spider net
With each breath a crashing desire to live
Like plants spreading their tendrils.

82
Ode to French Revolution

Storm was brewing to liberate
Against strict order, feuds, and trysts
French Revolution contravened the rigidity
Outburst of nimble creative energy with acuity.

Yo-Yo-ing thoughts of one's volition
Romanticism arose as a reaction to the revolution
Cosmic and elemental totems moved out of a luminal realm
As a stream of consciousness.

Poets unleashed into the creative enterprise
Literary works became a medium of expression
Truth and beauty made the dream a reality
Eclipsed inner dimensions started blooming.

Romanticism in conflict with the Enlightenment.
Illuminated ardent minds
Effectuated imaginative space
Free from the world's rigid gaze.

Sublime music of the sphere
Pirouetted around romance of the inner landscape
Brooding of golden eggs in all spheres
Spreading wings for the visionary quest.

83
Rainbow

A splash of rain
Felt the freshness of moist air
Sunlight strikes water crystal
Creates a splendid display of optical illusion.

Paints the sky with a dazzling glow
Of seven colors in a full circle
Glows in the far horizon
Forming a lovely arch or rainbow.

A physical metaphor of pure water crystal
Visualized in dream sequence
Evoked a sense of spirituality
Flying there to quench thirst.

84
Utopic Rhetoric

Life is full of tears and fears
Complicated mesh of emotion
Bound by the bounties of vagaries of fate
Sitting in a fragile boat in the stormy mid-sea.

Tantalizing spectrum
Unknown magic keeps hope alive
Wave of joy keeps the torments at bay
Magic of love offers secrets of existence.

With a fragile and visceral sense of longing
Lurking fear of the unknown veered away
Submersed in a state of relaxation and arousal
Felt deeply moving and fresh.

85
Voyage to Inner Landscape

Life is about creating memories
Accumulates an endless barrage of information
Perceived by sensory organs
Sculpt images of infinite contour
Through complex neuronal connectivity
Embedded in space and definite context
Somewhere deep in the soul
With silent endurance
Lasting and multiform imprint
All rambling thoughts – layers by layer
Clinching a permanent residence.
No mechanism to erase.

Memory and images – two veritable metaphors
A tantalizing combination of undefined topology
Intertwined in unknown dynamics
May or may not amount to a singular aura.
Converges somewhere in an unknown horizon
Oscillate in a bewildering complexity
Stridently eclipse one's conscious command
No one visualized ethereal metaphors
Only philosophers conjured
Its ineffable form

Guiding spirit of human intellect
All in haze
Solitary testimony of its own
Not common with anyone
Needs a master tool to access.

Strength and vitality of mental energy
Enamored with sweeping thoughts
Seeks a convenient route to navigate
Needs narrativize pictorial images into language
Demands a magic tool to translate
Wait for a glimpse of what's behind the curtain
Bright images are in the horizon.

Keep hope alive
Harness best of the present
Live with an infinite clear sky with a rainbow on the horizon
Enchanting and beautiful verdant shades of green
Blooming cherries and daffodils
Decorate soul with the grace of Virgil
Imagine Dante's vision of heaven where one would like to live.

86
Smile for Longing

Smiling makes one powerless to empowered
Silence the fractured dreams
Make peace with the barrage of variable thoughts
Resonate in tune with undulating waves
Anything from mundane to magical
With silent endurance
Feel the exhilarating sense of inner fullness.

Bathe in the buttery glow of nature's treasure-trove
Stoking trails of creative vision
Rising red disk of glorious sun
A tree, colorful butterflies, honey bees, and flowers
And the melody of songbird
Crystalline dew drops on a rose petal.

Water droplets of different sizes and shapes on leaves
Shower with smiling moonlight
Search for the "Star of Bethlehem" as Magi did
Navigate happily
Wherever mind goes
With enthralling sublimity.

87
"Land of Dilmun"

'Tree of knowledge' of good and evil
Singular totem of lifestream
Two extremes floating in a void
Embodies the beginning of conflict
Entry into a dystopic world of fragile terrain.

Zarathustra – central to ideas of dualism
Emblem of good and evil
Terrors and horrors
Tempestuous gains of truth
Spectrum of the human condition.

Nietzsche's intellectual introduction
Athenian tragedy – an art form of duality
Two "drives" rational & irrational
Named after Greek gods, Apollonian and Dionysian
Representing order and chaos.

In the ever-changing world
Two interwoven creative energies
Symphony of celestial revelation
Coupling of rational and irrational
Through which great art is born.

88
Random Thoughts

A gnawing creative cry
Something aspiring and elegance
Levees of passions and paradoxes
With full of ineptitude.

Where to go from here – I wonder
Ventures into an audacious goal
Success is always questionable
Until the finish line is crossed.

Edifies unbridled array of unknown emotion
Evolving from a deep, undefined horizon
Let the images be surfaced unobtrusive
A state of arousal, not relaxation.

World seemed under grand complexity
Shades of hope and despair in tandem
Generate a brand of magic
Between them lies the world of literature and art.

89
Way to Joy Land

Alone and singularly free
With a chainless mind
Carnival of new thoughts
Suddenly, a message arrives from distant star.

Evokes narratives of lovey-dovey homilies
Feeling of reverie enough to tuck away stasis
Everything became paradisal
Cardinal tenet of emotive enterprise.

Unaware that a poet sitting silently deep inside
Dialogue with inner world now perceptible
Imprints of beautifully lit objects
Gradually drifting to ashore with new meaning.

Enjoying the grace of distant star
Larger picture of good and beautiful
Something infinite behind everything
The eternal spirit of chainless mind.

90
Inner Balance

Perpetual balancing of the inner and outer world
Can it ever be harmonized?
Microcosm of grand complexity
A terrible precarious balancing act.

Symphony of hope and despair
Softness and vulnerability
Sliding between two extremes
Transfiguring experiences something luminous and sublime.

Chasms of obvious realities of life surface
Blurred boundaries vanishing
Thoughts mirror a fresh new perspective
Enough to drive away a cloud of uneasiness.

91
Memories of Ageing Father

First time in my arms
Witty, mischievous, with moony innocence
Created an invisible paradisal bond
Years are amazing, wonderous and gratifying.

Time passed by like the "Four seasons of Vivaldi"
Portrayal of variegated life course
Gradual transition from youth to manhood
Released from the vortex of father's mirthful eyes.

Every winter, this day memories return
A vivid portrayal of your journey
All are stacked in the mental diary
So much lovey-dovey.

Portentous vibrant flashbacks
Thoughts mirror a fresh new perspective
Memories inextricably woven together
We continue to be good friends.

92
Trances

Brain receives inputs during the stay in the mother's womb
Signals are either good or bad
Learning, a process of Pavlovian conditioning
Imprints in neuronal circuitry.

Connecting countless dots in our brain
Stay in the form of memory or knowledge
Expressed as imaginary
Either in a positive or negative form.

Thoughts waxes and wanes like wanderers
Originates from an unknown horizon of the brain
One wonders how waves originate
To act on the defined commend with precision.

Bungled attempt to understand life's great conundrum
Culmination of coding and decoding process
As a parable of one's inner journey
Acceptable revelation of mysteries of our existence.

93
Bond of Love

Wife trying to save her Covid husband
Mouth-to-mouth resuscitation
From impending death
Scene is chaotic and overwhelming.

Strength of emotion and pain
Importance of one's love for the dear one
His body gradually fades away
But her mind refuses to give up.

Signifying a bond – a permanent bond
A stark illustration
Something esoteric, understood by only chosen two
Choreographed something resonant, esoteric, and heavenly.

94
Light in the Dark

Interweaving of expressive imaginary
Subtle and unresolved
An account of inner life – connecting past and present
A complex imaginative savagery.

Unflinching description of the inner resonance
Ethos of exposing personal experiences
Subtle monologue of finding resilience and hope
In tune with the everchanging color of the universe.

Swimming in the perfect azure
Great moment for the alchemical act
Touch to transform inner desire into art
A trove of surreal poems with philosophical verse.

95
Liminal Space

Memories like an unwritten diary
Pops up as one grows old
Tender breeze scrolls pages one after another
Everything starts coming as redolent.

Huddles together in different shapes and sizes
May or may not in tenderly etched forms
In an unknown site of the brain
Resonates at different resonance.

The lyrics creating a dreamlike space
Incantatory celestial revelations
Enough to soothe the inner soul
Flying like a bird in my dream.

Gazing upwards to catch the rainbows
Made up of pure water crystals
Scope to quench one's thirst
The place where one would like to belong.

96
Four Seasons

Mapped distinctive color of each season
Hue of either warm or cool or a combination
Evokes lustrous, impeccable musical tenor
Feel of Vivaldi's four seasons.

Recalling John Keats, "The Human Seasons"
Youth as clear in spring, and manhood of summer
Middle age, like autumn – quiet life and decay in old age
represents winter
Reinforces perpetual bond between humans and
environment.

In the natural world, each period having different feelings
In Wordsworth's "Immortality ode"
Metamorphose as age advances
Old memories remain a moving connection between now
and then.

97
"Pieta"

Greatest epitome of the Renaissance
Michelangelo's "Pieta"
Crushing emotion
Of utter sadness and devastation.

Resigned to the event and graceful acceptance
Fragility of a mother carrying dead son on her lap
Pain is clear as the mother lost her son
Mother looking at her lost child.

Philosophers posited as a sublime experience
Dichotomy of her pain and peace
Strong push and pull between two emotions
Universal truth of mother and child relation.

A source of new research in neurobiology
"Archetype" imprint somewhere in the inner self
Whether operate autonomously or something genetic
Remains an open question to resolve.

Maybe a priori inherited psychic structures
A component of mind
Developed due to accumulated experience
Offering credence to "Jungian Psychology."

98
Numbness to Un-Numb

Lurid carnival of tormenting melodies
Darkness caused somatic shivering
A new shade of grey
Resistant to easy analysis.

Only a few courageous to delve into inner meaning
Whose eyes not clouded with tears
No smokescreen in deliberate use
Lacking lurking fear of sufferings.

Having enduring sensitivities
Enforcing re-sensitization to overcome deadliness
As in 'Magic Mountain' – hero started inner journey
Self-inoculation with the thoughts of suffering.

Thrived to overcome stagnation
Chekhov – a clinician, traveled to Sakhalin Island, a penal colony
Caught in the mist of pale view of suffering
Grand scenes of turning numbness to un-numb.

99
On a Distant Hilltop

With a gulping breathlessness
Keep gazing upwards
Toward the tip of a distant hilltop
Richly hued with flowers, foliage, sparrows, and butterflies.

Wildflowers bending toward the glowing sun
Soothing, meditative, and elegant
Recipe for joy in life stream
Matching the image of a pre-figuring vision of heaven.

Enshrined with bright colors as move upwards
So many colorful songbirds around
The wild world of music
Beautifully rendered.

Sense of uniqueness
Striking chiaroscuro portrait
Full of rhymes and resonances
Wake up with a peaceful mind.

New feelings with different contours born silently.

Life is growing up queer and surrounded by despair
Unwanted thoughts and creative enterprise run in tandem
Fleeting new thoughts surfaced with a tinge of color
Offering a new tool to create next move.

From the mass of blurry mesh
Emerges erudite sensibility of the self
Desirous to express inner landscape in language
Symbolic promise of transformation.

Countless forms of mixed memories surfaced from murky depth
Wave of thoughts appear and disappear, how they originate
Honoring memory, left with a way forward
Wail of anguish fueled intellectual organism.

Broken and wounded, laden with a sense of survival
Thoughts, rich in liturgical chants – a source of new self
Perhaps the darkness is gradually lifting
There wasn't much more one can ask for.

Suffering became my best friend
Transforming darkness into the grace of early spring
Source of new artistic inspiration
Conformity with a robust appetite for living.

Stimulus to transfigure loss into creativity
Nested deep inside a priceless gem
Beyond the perceived world
Something of sensorial abundance.

100
War in Brain

Unexpected windfall of poignancy and an ache
Discord between memory and forgetting
Portentous flashback of past torments
Opens terrines of fundamental uncertainties.

Memories exist in a kind of mental desk-top
As representation of the past events
Move hither and thither beyond the boundaries of self-control
Deserves to be unpacked and to be aired with candor.

Lying in an empathy and ethery tearful state of mind
Hopelessly trembling over the edge of the void
Near demise of hope
Elegiac, but enshrined with a sense of survival.

Mind keeps the score of each event
Inscribed in the primal part of the brain
A doomsday of spiral discord of unspecified composition
Kneaded in a self-contained blueprint.

Why certain experiences lodged in memories
Some others are barely traceable
Testament of evolution of inner complex world